For Jonathan
Christmas 1987
With our love. Mom + Dad
Xx

Standing on a Strawberry

AF470724

JOHN CUNLIFFE

Illustrated by David Parkins

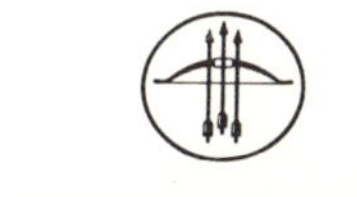

ANDRE DEUTSCH

First published 1987 by
André Deutsch Limited
105–106 Great Russell Street, London WC1B 3LJ

Text copyright © 1987 by John Cunliffe
Illustrations copyright © 1987 by David Parkins
All rights reserved.

British Library Cataloguing in Publication Data

Cunliffe, John
Standing on a strawberry.
I. Title II. Parkins, David
821′914 PR6053.U4/

ISBN 0 233 98071 7

Photoset by Rowland Phototypesetting Limited
Bury St Edmunds, Suffolk

Printed and bound in Great Britain by
WBC Bristol and Maesteg

To a slug, crawling up my milk-bottle.

Now, Mr. Slug,
I don't want you on my milk,
nor any of your ilk!

A bug
in a rug
may be snug,

But a slug on a bottle,
stops my glottle.

Transformations

It was a tale of spells I told;
'Is it true?' she said,
'Is it true?'
The child's eyes grew round with every telling;
And still she asked,
'Is it true?
'Is it really true?
'Can the pumpkin turn into a coach?
'Can the frog become a prince?'

Then I thought of transformations
I have seen
Or heard tell of:
Of boys become men,
And men grown old:
Of new blossom, falling leaf,
And, again, new blossom,
Year to year.
'Yes,' I said, 'it is true.
'In its way,
It is true.'

Sardicarus

A baby sardine
In a flying machine
Flew much too near to the sun.
Said his mum,
'It's ridiculous,
You're not Icarus!'
'No,' said the kid,
'but it's fun.'

Standing on a Strawberry

'You're standing on a strawberry,'
I heard the teacher say.
It was an end-of-term school dinner,
and we'd had strawberries that day.
'You're standing on a strawberry,
and it isn't very good,
to put your great big feet,
on what's left of someone's pud!'

'You're sitting on a sausage,
and you're making such a mess,
that when you get home tonight
your mum will never guess,
what on earth you have been up to
to get in such a state.
It really is much better,
to keep your dinner on a plate.'

'You have your elbow in the custard,
and it's soaking up your sleeve.
Such a mess you're making,
that no human could believe
one little bowl of custard,
could go so very far,
and I promise you, my lad,
you'll get a roasting from your ma.'

'You're slurping up the soup,
and you're spilling half your peas.
There's a pencil and a ball-pen
embedded in the cheese.
Someone's dropped a plastic spider,
into the orange juice.'
The teacher shouts for silence,
but it isn't any use.

It's just another dinner-time
and it's very nearly done.
The battle of the servers
has been fought, and lost, and won.
You scatter to the playground
where you run so wild and free,
whilst the teachers, in the staffroom,
have a quiet cup of tea.

Another Assembly

The old man mounts the platform;
(If you have not been this way,
You have never known true boredom.)
What is the theme for today?
He will ravel up his rigmarole . . .
Dirty toilets,
Lost coats,
Noisy children,
Broken pencils,
Torn books,
Swimming certificates.

Hands together,
Eyes closed,
EYES CLOSED,
EVERYONE.
We pray – oh, how we pray,
For fire to descend from heaven,
And consume him to the last syllable.
But . . . no chance,
He will lead us, yet, a merry dance,
For now we are lost in the day's theme,
From THE PRIMARY TEACHER'S ASSEMBLY
BOOK.
But, what is this?
We have drifted unawares;
We are now in a colonial African school,
Surrounded by distant tribes,
Who received his diatribes,
Twenty years ago;
And all is mysteriously linked
With a silver hand-bell,
Which he tinkles at us.
And how did he get from there,
To the sinking of the Titanic?

This sadly tangled thread,
(We lost our grip on it long since)
Fills us only with the dread,
That it may have no ending.
But now we are singing Number Twenty-Six,
Passing hymn-books,
Filing out.
We hear his parting shout,
At some unfortunate lout;
Relieved, we run to class or play,
Happy in the thought;
Assembly is over for another day.

Girls

We've all sorts of girls in our school:
Bony,
Podgy,
Giggly,
Dodgy,
Sickly smiley,
Shampooed and shiny,
Smelly wellies,
Big and busty,
Dirty dusty;
All sorts . . .
Some pretty ones, too . . .
One or two really nice ones . . .
Well . . . one, just one . . . really special one.
BUT
The one I really hate,
Is Miss Whisper-behind-her-hand.
She gives me a smooth look,
Snooty;
Then she whispers to her Special Friend,
And I know it's something nasty,
. . . about me.

Standing Up to Read a Poem In Front of All These People

I've got to do it,
Sir says so,
And we've been practising
For weeks.
We missed games last night,
To have a
Final Rehearsal.
I've got to do it,
Because Sir's picked me,
And mam says she'll be proud,
But Sir says NOT TOO LOUD
And don't rush it;
But I feel sure
I'll mess it up.
It'll be all right
If I remember how it should go,
And our Jim doesn't pick his nose,
In the front row,
And make me laugh.
So here goes . . .
....
Damn.................
How does it begin?

Cat Warmth

All afternoon,
My cat sleeps,
On the end of my bed.

When I creep my toes
Down between the cold sheets,
I find a patch of cat-warmth
That he's left behind;
An invisible gift.

Riddle

I like to sit,
In a warm place;
I breathe water,
And sing with it,
Then scream
Until
You pull my nose off.

[Answer on page 14.]

Pebbles

We collect days,
Like a boy collecting pebbles
On the beach.

Suddenly his pockets are heavy.

Suddenly, we are old.

The Teacher

Thirty years
of pretended surprise,
Have brought
an artificial glitter to her eyes;
A brittle brightness
to her voice,
That you would flee from,
if you had the choice.

Morning Assembly

A funeral passed the school,
Whilst the recorder group
Played for assembly.
Later, careers were discussed;
A small child said,
'I'll be a doctor when I grow up,
and help dead people.'

[Answer to the riddle: A kettl

Silent Susan

Susan, silent,
Amid the mob
Of infants.

She rarely speaks,
And then
In the faintest whisper.

What moves
Behind those eyes?
Those dark pools,
Brown as
Peat-water
In a moorland pond.

A lonely place,
Calm amid turmoil.

Billy Boils

Billy simmers,
Billy boils,
Red hair,
Flames,
Topping fiery thoughts.

Outraged by . . .
Maths,
Writing,
Drawing,
Discussion,
Story Time,
Projects,
And hymns,
Most of all by hymns!

Such indignities!

Billy, grown up,
Will maintain a head of steam,
Faced by . . .
Tax-demands,
VAT,
Bills for . . .
Rent,
Rates,
Electricity,
Gas,
Telephone,
Car,
Kids,
Wife,
Parking-tickets,
Fines,
Final Demands.

Such indignities!

Two Teams

Garry plays in two teams,
The football team,
And the poetry team.

He scored last week;
Wrote a poem
About Maggy Thatcher's
Blackpool trip,
In 2001.
I didn't know
He saw such a fallen world.

He scored again last week,
With an amazing goal.
I didn't know
You could get the ball
In at such an angle.

Garry plays in two teams,
And he's a great shot in both.

Canny Newt

Can a newt
Play Canute?
No – the tide,
Is far too wide.
It would take him
For a ride.
Canny newt,
Not to moot,
Such a route!

Fish

fat
cat
swish
fish

purr
fur
wish
fish

paw
below
dip
flip

mouth
wide
fish
slip
slide
inside

lips
lick
cat
nap

God Called Round Last Night

Who made the world?
Was it God?
'I'm not sure,' I said,
'I'm not sure that he exists.'
'I am,' said Sheryl,
'I know he does.'
(So sure, and only eight.)
'How do you know?'
'I've seen him.
He called at our house
last night.'
'Why did he call?'
'I don't know.'
'What did he look like?'
'Tall, with a grey beard.'
She could be right.
Well, she could.
Who's to say?

Do You Want to Hear My Poem?

(said the poet to his wife)

Well, not right now,
My egg's coming to the boil,
My toast's burning,
I have a bus to catch,
I haven't done my hair,
My make-up's all wrong,
My shoe's too tight,
I have to hang the washing out,
The phone's ringing,
I have a lot of shopping,
My pencil's broken,
I can't find my keys,
Where is my purse?
Do you want to hear my poem?
Not just now!

The Selective Cat

The selective cat,
When offered a rat,
Said, 'It really isn't me,
I can't abide rat,
And that is that,
I'd rather have *ratatouile*.'

The Summer Show

There will be a great flying display,
Not to be missed,
In my garden,
To-morrow,
From dawn onwards.
Two swallows,
Promise to make a summer of it,
The magpies will provide a commentary,
From the upper branches of the birch tree,
Whilst the sparrows
Will make stand-by flights,
From gutter to gutter.
Don't miss it!

On What Stage

At the door of the Palace Theatre,
He greets well-to-do Mancunians,
With his 'Good Luck!' message,
Felt-penned on a piece of card,
And spoken, wooden-faced,
Like a Punch-and-Judy figure.
'Good Luck!' from one who seems to have little,
To those who seem to have enough and more.
Tunes from the evening's opera,
Wheeze out from his accordion.
A small nest of coins in his cap,
Gleams in the expensive lamp-light.

Where does he go when the curtain rises?
On what stage does his drama unfold?

On Driving Behind a Funeral at Fifteen Miles an Hour

Why do funerals go so slow?
I don't know.

Why is it wrong to hurry,
On the way to bury?

To be an overtaker
Of an undertaker,
Seems *infra dig*,
Though it cannot be a big
Deal to the dead,
When the soul has fled.

It must be those who weep,
Who like to keep
A pace so dignified and slow;
Knowing *this* is the way
that they
will go.

Epitaphs

ON A BUS CONDUCTOR

Here lies the conductor
Of a forty-one bus;
At last he's reached
His terminus.

ON A WEAVER

She was not deft,
With her weft,
Now she winds her warp,
To the sound of a harp.

Late Comers

There's a special club
In our school;
The late-comers club.

They catch slow buses
From distant places,
Never have alarm-clocks,
Always have excuses,
Wonderful excuses!

In assembly,
They sit in a bunch,
Just inside the door,
Pretending not to exist.

They grow up to be;
Glib of tongue,
Never, seemingly, in the wrong;
Novelists;
Television script-writers;
Antique dealers;
Politicians.

Such are the benefits,
Of creative excuse-making.

Teacher Says

Teacher says RIGHT
Teacher says WRONG
How does she *know*?
Where does she go,
For all the answers?
Is *she* ever marked WRONG;
Made to stand outside;
Write five hundred lines;
Sing hymns;
When she doesn't feel like it?

School

School is a place
Where you have to go,
Where they tell you things
You don't want to know.
Where children scream
and teachers shout,
and life can be ruled
by a bullying lout.

Telephoning Teacher

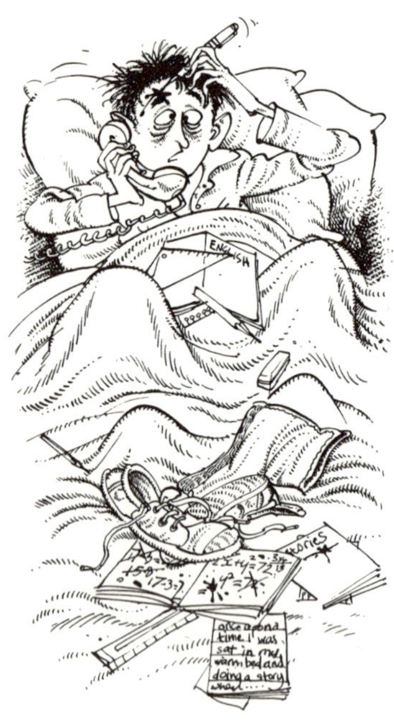

Teacher! Teacher!
I'm having trouble with my story!
It starts quite well,
But the ending's gory.
Teacher! Teacher!
I'm having trouble with my sums!
I'm running out of fingers,
I'm running out of thumbs!
Teacher! Teacher!
I'm having trouble with P.E.!
I've a crick in my shoulder,
A pain in my knee!
Teacher! Teacher!
I feel a proper fool!
Teacher! Teacher!
I don't like school!
Teacher! Teacher!
I can't come today!
I'll get my mum to write a note,
So I can stop away.
Teacher! Teacher!
Don't be cross,
Teacher! Teacher!
I don't give a toss.
I don't go at all for this learning lark,
I'd rather go and wag it in the park.
Teacher! Teacher!
It's no use!
I'll think up
A marvellous excuse.
My eyes are crossed,
And my legs are lead,
And I'm going to stay,
All day,
In bed.

Note:
in Manchester, "wag it," means, "play truant."

Calling The Doctor

Doctor! Doctor!
I've got trouble with my nose!
Doctor! Doctor!
I've got trouble with my toes!
Doctor! Doctor!
I've got trouble with my head!
Doctor! Doctor!
I'm stopping in bed!

Quick! Get a Builder!

Builder! Builder!
My house's falling!
Builder! Builder!
It's quite appalling!
The roof's blown off,
And the rain's coming in!
And I'm going to go
And live in the bin!

An urgent call to the dentist

Dentist! Dentist!
I've got toothache!
It's like the bite of a poison-snake!
Dentist! Dentist!
Do something quick!
I'm very very very sick.
Dentist! Dentist!
Pull it out!
I promise, honest,
I will not shout!
I don't even care,
If I have to pay,
I'll get on the bike,
And come right away.

Ouch! Stoppit!
Blood and thunder!
Dentist! Dentist!
You've made a blunder!
And just look how
My blood keeps spurting!
And I do believe,
My tooth's still hurting!
Dentist! Dentist!
I tell the truth!
You've gone and pulled . . .
You've pulled the wrong tooth!

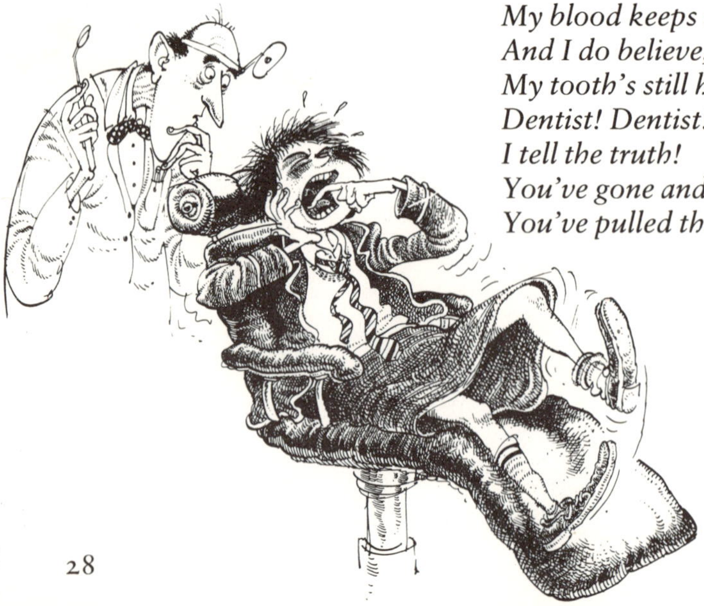

Ringing the Missus

Wife! Wife!
The baby's crying,
The pudding's burnt,
And the plants are dying!
The cat's been sick,
And the dog's lost his bone!
Wife! Wife!
You've gotta come home!

Grown Up?

When I'm grown up
What do I want to be?
Well, Sir,
Since you ask,
I wouldn't mind . . .
I wouldn't mind being a tree.
I'd like to push my feet
Into the soil,
And stand there,
A few hundred years,
Just *being* . . .
Just being a tree.

But if I can't be a tree,
I think I'd just like to be *bad*.
I'd like to have cakes and champagne in the
afternoon,
And eat condensed milk straight out of the tin,
With a green plastic spoon;
I'd have handmaidens bringing sherbet,
And a pet boa-constrictor called Herbert.
I'd lie on a silken divan,
Reading lurid novels,
And make fat profits,
From people in hovels;
I'd go to Oxford,
Take my teddy bear,
And dine on oysters and paté,
Gin and jugged hare.
I'd................
But he's not listening,
They never do . . .

One thing I'll *never* be,
When I grow up;
I'll never be,
A fat man,
In a pin-stripe suit;
Who smiles his fat smile,
At a pimply Second Year,
Lays a heavy hand
On the boy's shoulder,
And says,

'Now, young man,
What do you want to be,
When you grow up?'
Then walks away,
Without listening,
With a sneer and a wink
At the Head,
And a burst of coarse laughter
Down the corridor.

Crab

*C*rafty hunter
*R*acing slantways
*A*cross the shore:
*B*aleful bone-box.

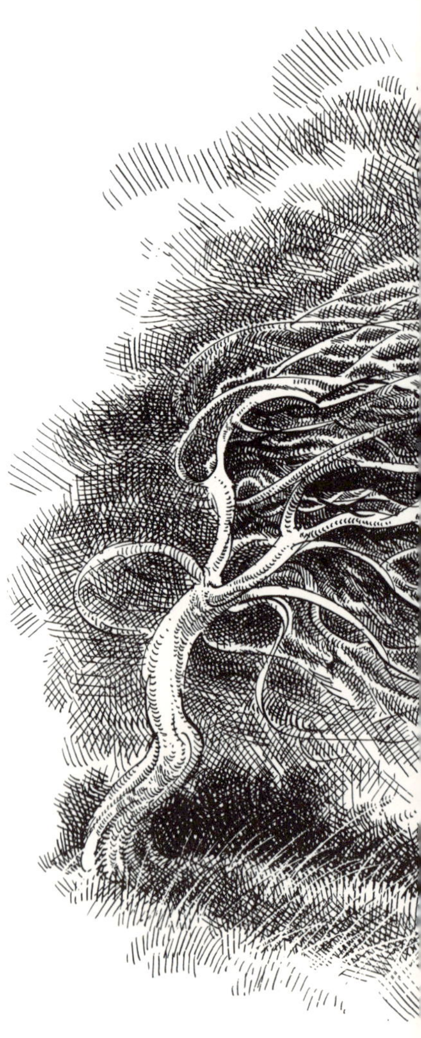

Willow in the Wind

The wind surges,
Seething through the tree,
Buffeting its branches,
So delicate to defy
This tenuous tide.
Trees tumble in full sail,
Brave mariners of the land.

The Wind in a Tree

The wind in a tree,
Makes a sound like the sea.

The branches are like breakers;
. . . *green* horses.

A Twitching in the Grass

I thought the garden
was a peaceful place,
until, one calm
and sunny morning,
I saw a twitching
in the grass.
A brown shape
lay spreadeagled
on its back.
At first, I thought,
'A fledgling fallen
from its nest?'
But, no, it was
not a thing of air,
it was a young frog,
its throat torn out
by a marauding magpie,
or the blackbird
that sings so beautifully
at dawn and dusk?

PS.
It's all right for you,
said the frog,
writing a poem about me!
I'm lying here with my throat ripped out,
and that's for real.
Poets, like magpies,
swoop upon
any tasty morsel.

Help!

Help! cried the man,
with the tank and the gun;
Help! he cried,
though the battle was won;
Silent, he was,
when he lay on the hill;
Silent because,
he had paid the bill.

He was . . .

He was . . .
a boy who became
a man
a husband
a father.

He was . . .
a good goalie,
a rotten batsman,
not bad at darts.

He was . . .
second cornet in the works band;
a man who brought his pay-packet straight home,
without stopping at the pub;
a man who enjoyed his dinner.

He was . . .
forgetful,
rarely on time,
sometimes tongue-tied
at a loss for what to say.

He was . . .
always honest,
never sober at Christmas,
often puzzled by the world.

He was . . .
my dad.

In Praise of Grans

I like grans,
Grans are good,
They never give you food
You don't like,
Or lock up your bike,
When you come in all covered in mud.
Grans are not in a hurry,
Grans don't worry
About exams;
Grans are grans,
And I like grans.

Grans United

Have you heard
Of Grans United?
I dare say you haven't,
As they've not been sighted,
All together at a match.
They sit quietly and hatch
Their plans
Behind a barricade,
Of knitting needles;
That's how grans'
Games are won.
Home or away,
Day by day.

The opposition is stiff at times;
Stiff joints – sore bones,
The injuries of extra time.
But they fight back,
With cups of sweet tea,
And bottles of bright capsules;
Games away – by coach to Blackpool,
Internationals, even,
In the cheap Spanish sun;
Bazaars, bingo, television, and toast,
By a warm fireside;
Church choirs and outings,
And, best of all,
Looked-forward-to all week
Visits from beloved grandchildren.
Sweets hoarded in a drawer,
Treasures saved and wrapped in tissue,
Treats and trinkets and surprises;
Secrets shared,
Confidences confided.
I support Grans United.

Asleep

A child said,
'There are people in our graveyard
who are not dead.
They are not dead at all,
but they are in graves.'

Ghosts?
Spooks?
Spectres?

I went to see for myself,
and there it was,
as plain as a pig!
The words were carved on the stone;
'In loving memory of Ethel,
Who fell asleep on the 13th May 1910.'
I listened for sounds of snoring,
but all was silent.
Plainly, Ethel was a quiet sleeper,
but what an odd place for a sleep!
And surely it must be true?
Who would carve a lie so deeply in stone?
I listened again,
but all was silent.
What about the church-bells?
Wouldn't they waken her?
Then what?
Then what?

The Mutinous Jack-in-a-box

Why should I always jump
when they press that stupid button?
Always at their call?
Next time . . . *next* time . . .
I'll stick my tongue out at them.
I'll spit!
I'll shout rude words!
I'll pull horrid faces!
I'll make their baby cry
and turn their milk sour.
I will!
Just you wait and see!
They can't fool me;
not forever a slave;
next time I'll be brave.

B O O O O O O O O I I I I N N N N N N N G G G G
G G G G G G G G G
!!!!!

Oh dear, I did it again,
Up I jumped,
Grinning as though I had no brain;
But . . . just you wait and see.
Next time I'll do it;
I will . . . I will . . .

Home Haircut

Nellie, cutting Johnnie's hair,
Was taking insufficient care;
She turned to hear what someone said,
And found that she'd cut off his head!
She smiled, 'I know just what to do,'
And stuck it on again with glue.

Riddles

1.

A city of thousands,
Yet no word is spoken.
There are great stores of gold,
But no money.
Some live imprisoned in cells,
Yet are good citizens.
Their six-legged cows,
give sweet milk;
They have no king –
But a queen rules and serves them.

2.

Soft shapes you can see,
But not touch.
They dim the day's eye,
Move silently,
Grow and die in an hour,
Travel the world,
Between scene and space.

Answers to the riddles on the previous page.

1. A bee-hive.

2. Clouds.

Orders of the Day

Get up!
Get washed!
Eat your breakfast!
That's my mum,
Going on and on and on and on . . .

Sit down!
Shut up!
Get on with your work!
That's my teacher,
Going on and on and on and on . . .

Come here!
Give me that!
Go away!
That's my big sister,
Going on and on and on and on . . .

Get off!
Stop it!
Carry me!
That's my little sister,
Going on and on and on and on . . .

Boss
Boss
Boss
They do it all day.
Sometimes I think I'll run away,
But I don't know
Where to go.

The only one who doesn't do it,
Is my old gran.
She says,
'Would you like to get washed?'
Or,
'Would you like to sit on this chair?'
And she listens to what I say.
People say she spoils me,
And that she's old-fashioned.
I think it's the others that spoil;
They spoil every day.
And I wish more people were old-fashioned,
. . . like my gran.

Thoughts about Princess Diana and a box of chocolates

I wonder if Diana,
Would like to chuck a spanner
in the middle of the Royal Jamboree?

Would she like to munch a box
of '*oh-so-fattening*' chocs,
or spend a weekend down in Brighton
on a spree?

When she shakes a thousand hands,
or listens to brass bands,
would she rather put her feet up
with a book?

Would she rather watch the telly,
play a disc of old Lead Belly,
be a teacher, or a preacher, or a cook?

With folks like you and me,
when you're going out to tea,
you can go to Harrods, or a Wimpy down the street.
But it must be very hard,
with a six-man bodyguard,
to nip out to a chippy for a treat.

I really think that Di
would often like to fly
to a place where no one knows her royal name,
where she'd forget all fame and wealth,
and really be herself.
But she can't do it.
What a rotten shame!

I Wish I Was an Infant

I wish I was an infant
in the class of Mrs. Bell,
If I ever felt unhappy,
I'm sure she'd make me well.
She'd tell me lots of stories,
And teach me how to read,
And have a plaster handy,
If my leg began to bleed.
I'd feel like someone special,
Each time she smiled at me,
And I'd think I was in heaven,
When she sat me on her knee.
I wish I was an infant
in the class of Mrs. Bell;
If I ever felt unhappy,
I'm sure she'd make me well.

Mr Way

Mr. Way lived
In a hideaway house,
With a tearaway dog,
And a slip-away mouse.

Ate a take-away meal,
In a throwaway box,
Wore a cut-away suit,
And give-away socks.

Took put-away cash,
From an out of way bank,
Jumped a getaway cab
From a taxi-rank.

Mr. Way,
Clear away,
Out for fun,
Made a stowaway trip,
To a faraway sun.

Mr. Way's 'Gone Away',
For ever ever more,
So it's no use knocking,
On his hideaway door.

Mr. Way!
Oh, Mr. Way!
He's gone away for ever,
And I'm sure you'll never find him,
Unless you're very clever.

Snow Thoughts

What does a snowman eat?
What does a snowman drink?
What does a snowman dream?
What does a snowman think?

Ball-Bounce Rhyme

Let's catch a bus
And go to town,
And ride the escalators
Up and down.

Up and down
And home again,
Jumping puddles
In the rain.

Home to chips
And a cup of tea,
Watching films
On the old tv.

The Ballad of Johnny Shiner; a story for harvest festival.

This is the tale
Of Johnny Shiner,
Born in the year
Of forty-nine;
With brothers and sisters,
Three, four, five,
It was good to be alive;
In the sun and wind
To run.
Life a game
And full of fun.

Johnny grew up
And went to school,
And soon his head
Was teeming full,
Of sums and art
And other goodies,
And environmental
Studies!
'Whatever's that?'
Said Mum and Dad;
'It's about our world,'
Said the promising lad.
'The things we need
To live and grow,
Earth's good store
From the crops we sow,
The harvest of
The sea and land,
Blessed by the
Almighty's hand.

Johnny did well,
He did not shirk,
School was finished,
Time for work.
Out into
The world of men,
Stepped our clever
Johnny then.
'What shall I do,
With my arm so strong,
To help the folks
I live among?
Where is the work,
Fit to my hand,
To make life good
In our fair land?'

Johnny Shiner,
Johnny Shiner,
You shall go
To be a miner.

Johnny joined
His fellow men,
Stepped in the cage,
And the gate clashed, then,
Down he dropped
Into the earth,
And Johnny he prayed
For all his worth;
'Please God bring me
Safe again,
Into the sun
And wind
And rain.'

Johnny picked up
His pick and lamp,
Crouched down low
In the dark and damp.
Hacked at the coal
In a three-foot seam,
Thought school and childhood
Just a dream.

Seven long years
Our Johnny worked,
Never faltered
Never shirked.
Then came the word
On the news at nine,
FIFTY MINERS
TRAPPED DOWN THE MINE.
Johnny, wakened
From a dream,
Rushed to join
The rescue team.
They dug out forty
Safe and sound,
But ten were lost
Deep underground.
And later,
When the names were read,
Johnny knew his
Friend was dead.

So Johnny he up
And walked away,
To live and fight
Another day.
'I'll work,' said he,
'In the sun and the rain,
My harvest to be
The golden grain.'

Then Johnny Shiner
Prayed to the Lord,
'Oh let your people
Hear the word,
The sun and the rain
Are all we need,
With the fertile earth
And the growing seed,
The wind and the river,
That flows from the hills,
Can give us power
And turn our mills.
The harvest of lives
In the murderous mine,
Can be no part
Of a plan of thine.
Let us harvest the earth
Yet keep it whole,
For earth is precious,
Earth is small.'

And Johnny Shiner
Said Amen.
And Johnny Shiner
Said Amen.

A Pop-Star at Forty

His gear hangs in the wardrobe,
all the crowds have gone away,
and when he goes down the dole-queue,
he's stuck for what to say;
An out-of-work pop-singer,
out of luck, and out of cash;
Though once, in silver lurex,
he'd cut a mighty dash;
He'd have the ravers screaming,
from London to Southend;
But, as he gazed into the spotlight,
he knew there'd be an end;
An end to all the glamour,
of being on the scene;
It would make him, and it would break him,
the Super-Star machine.
He would step into the shadows,
with Garry, Steve, and Jim;
O was there – just – a chance,
that it wouldn't come to him?
Could he cling to fame and glory,
maybe cut a Golden Disc?
There was a glittering world to grasp at,
and he'd have to take the risk.

So off he went on tour,
round Europe and the States;
Following in the footsteps,
of all the All-Time Greats;
Like the Stones, the Who, the Beatles,
and good old Leo Sayer,
He went from gig to gig,
on a song and on a prayer;
He prayed for fans and money,
that would never never stop;

That he'd go into the charts,
and stay forever at the top.

It seemed his prayers were answered,
for a company signed him on;
And he appeared on the telly,
in a show with Elton John;
The dollars they flowed in,
and the dollars they flowed out;
He endured a hundred concerts,
with rave, and stomp, and shout;
He made a double-album,
that went climbing up the charts;
His sad songs and his love-songs,
captured teenage hearts;
They sent him sacks of fan-mail,
full of love that would not die;
At last he was the Greatest,
brightest pop-star in the sky.
Top of all the charts,
and spangled with success;
The ending of the story,
something he could never guess.

He didn't take to drink,
and drugs were not his scene;
He didn't wear out his talent,
on the celebrity machine;
He didn't hit the headlines,
in a motorway smash;
He didn't get religion,
with a message brief and brash.
The fashion swiftly changed,
like an unrelenting fate;
Just when his act was perfect,
he was – simply – out of date!
There was a new group in the spotlights,
and new faces at the top;

New makers of success,
that could never never stop.
He dropped out of the charts,
and never left a trace;
Well, who wants to know
yesterday's face?

An out-of-work pop-singer,
out of luck, and out of cash;
Though once, in silver lurex,
he'd cut a mighty dash;
The fans have all departed,
and left a nasty taste;
Was it *ever* worth it,
or was it – just – a – waste?

Alpha – B375 – EARTH VISITOR'S GUIDE..........SECTION 789/3556776621000oA»DF

....

(This text has been transcribed and translated, using a Titan B789000 computer, from the Alphan computer printout. This was found in the wreckage of a space-vehicle, discovered in the Himalayas, in 2080. Only a few fragments of a much longer document survived the disastrous fire which destroyed all life-forms on the vehicle.)

....
....

Galactic Government Health Warning.
Earth is a high-risk planet,
And is to be visited
Only with the greatest caution.

Seen though a telescope,
You may think
Earth a lovely planet.
Alphan travellers are warned,
This is pure deception.
Earth is tricky,
In places, toxic,
And earth-dwellers
Are not to be trusted,
Being primitive and untamed
Members of the galaxy;
Violent polluters
Of their own biosphere.
Earth is as bizarre a planet,
As any in the universe.

How to Exchange Data With Earth-men

Earth-men are beginning to learn
To use computers for communication,
But much data-transfer is done
By a primitive method,
Long forgotten on Alpha – B375.
This uses a gaseous medium
To transmit a pattern
Of low-frequency vibrations,
Over a short distance.
This pattern is coded and decoded
Into a series of non-digital signals,
Which yet can carry meaning,
When received by head-organs,
Long defunct in Alphans.

You will need several megabytes
Of computer memory,
To store and decode
The patterns used,
In addition to
Complex hardware and software.

Earth-men call this system,
SPEECH.

To make matters worse,
Differing patterns are used
In different parts of Earth.
Earth-men call this system,
LANGUAGE.

Being complex, vague, and uncertain,
Many coding and decoding errors
Are produced by these systems.
Earth-men call these errors,
MISUNDERSTANDINGS.

Now you will understand
Why earth-men are forever fighting.

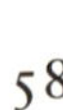

Further systems have been observed,
Using sustained vibrations,
At regular intervals,
With repeated patterns,
Some with a mathematical basis.
It is not known why
Earth-men use these.
At times they seem
To have a calming effect,
At other times to excite,
And cause the Earth-men
To move in strange ways,
Even to laugh or weep.
The Earth-men call these systems,
MUSIC and POETRY.

From this you will see,
What a strange planet
Earth can be.

Alpha B375 – RESIDENT'S HANDBOOK

Gardening on Alpha B375 can be hazardous.
Scrots are a good but grim example.
They flourish well by earthlight,
But must be eaten within one month
From the appearance of the fruit;
If you leave them a day longer,
They will eat *you*!

Many a weary gardener,
Has fought a losing battle,
At the end of a miscalculated month.

Talking Lettuce

A new variety has been bred;
It has crisp, tasty leaves,
And it speaks English.
Don't let it go to seed;
It will then spread chatterboxes,
All over your garden,
And you will get no peace,
Day or night.
Our mental hospitals are full
Of cases of chatterbox infestation.

Musical Rhubarb

This is the latest example of
Cross-breeding with an earth-plant.
You can eat it,
Or play it!
Be careful not to eat too much.
One lady did so;
She passed melodious wind,
In the key of C-sharp minor,
In the middle of a symphony-concert,
Leaving the orchestra
Off-key for the rest of the evening.

Speculum
Opticalis ....

This herb is a great money-saver.
With careful cultivation,
It will produce –
Spectacles,
Telescopes,
Magnifiers,
Opera-glasses,
Microscopes.
A special variegated variety,
Produces bifocals,
Whilst Speculum Opticalis Polaroidus,
Gives a good crop of sunglasses,
If it gets plenty of sunshine.
Crossed with clinging pond-weed,
It makes passable contact-lenses.

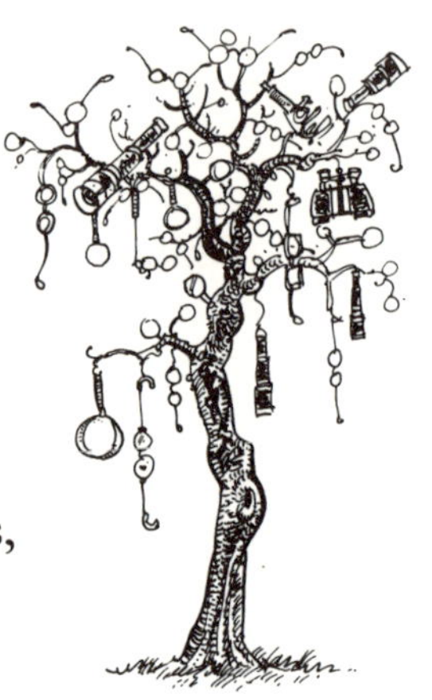

....

....

Illustrated
Cabbage ....

This entertaining vegetable
Grows in many varieties.
It will colour your dreams
In the most startling ways.
It can be used as wallpaper,
Or, shredded, woven into carpets.
Take care with Briggs Beauty.
Colourful and humorous it may be,
But it is subject to fungus diseases.

Carrots (High Octane)

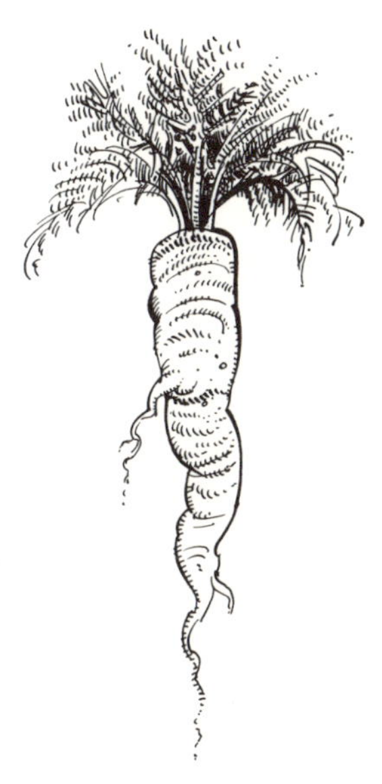

Earth-carrots grow strangely
On Alpha B375.
Their high-octane content
Is stupendous!
Do *not* eat them;
In contact with digestive juices
They explode.

Put them in the fuel-tank
Of your hover-car,
And hold your helmet.
A hover-racer,
Carrot-fuelled,
Went into orbit last year,
And had to wait a week
For a shuttle to bring him down.

Another Day

Boys shout,
Girls giggle,
Pencils write,
Squiggle squiggle.
Get it wrong,
Cross it out,
Bell's gone!
All out!

Balls bounce,
Hands clap,
Skipping ropes,
Slap slap.
Hand-stands,
By the wall,
Sara Williams
Best of all.
Boys fight,
Girls flee,
Teacher's gone
And spilt
His tea!
Clatter bang!
Big din!
Whistle goes,
All in!

All quiet,
No sound,
Hear worms,
Under ground.
Chalk squeaks,
Clock creeps,
Head on desk,
Boy sleeps.

Home time!
Glory be!
Mum's got
Chips for tea.
Warm fire,
Full belly,
Sit down,
Watch telly.

Bed time,
Creep away,
Dream until,
Another day.